British
Grand Prix Heroes

British
Grand Prix Heroes

TIM HILL

Photographs by LAT

p

Above: Clark, Cooper, Ireland, Moss, Hill, Bonnier, McLaren,
Gurney at the 1961 German Grand Prix, Nurburgring.
Page One: The King and future Queen meet drivers Stirling Moss
and Peter Collins at the 1950 British Grand Prix, Silverstone.

This is a Parragon book
This edition published in 2006

Parragon
Queen Street House
4 Queen Street
Bath BA1 1HE, UK

All photographs © LAT
Text © Parragon Books Ltd 2005
Produced by Atlantic Publishing

A catalogue record for this book is available from the British Library.

ISBN 1 40546 730 4
Printed in China

British
Grand Prix Heroes

Cliff Allison

Born 8 February 1932 (Brough, Cumbria)
Grand Prix starts: 16   Grand Prix victories: 0   Points total: 11

A sparkling career cut short by injury.

Cliff Allison's racing career began as a 20-year-old in Formula Three, where he made steady progress, finishing fourth in the 1955 championship. That year he became works driver for Lotus sports cars, Colin Chapman's outfit, still two years away from developing single-seaters.

The Lotus 12 first appeared in 1957, the year Allison made a name for himself with an Index of Performance win at Le Mans.

Allison fronted Lotus' world championship debut in 1958, partnering Graham Hill. Although both suffered a string of retirements it was Allison who made the greater impact. After two 6th places he finished a fine 4th at Spa. Then, in the new Lotus 16, he ran brilliantly at the Nurburgring and might have won had his radiator remained intact.

Second to McLaren

His promising performances caught the eye of Ferrari, and in 1959 he joined the Prancing Horse team, albeit as one of the second string supporting Jean Behra and Tony Brooks. Fifth place in Monaco was his best return for that season, but he opened his 1960 campaign with an excellent 2nd to Bruce McLaren at the Argentinian Grand Prix. He crashed in practice for round two, Monaco, suffering a badly broken arm when he was catapulted from his Ferrari. That brought a premature end to his season.

Leg injury ends career

In 1961 Allison returned to F1 with the UDT Laystall team, which was running the old Lotus 18. In the curtain-raiser, Monaco, he finished a creditable 8th, two places ahead of Jim Clark in Lotus' new 21 model. It was to be his sixteenth and final Grand Prix, for he crashed during practice for Spa, sustaining leg injuries which ended his career.

Allison with Henry Taylor at the 1961 Belgian Grand Prix.

Bob Anderson

19 May 1931 (London) - 14 August 1967
Grand Prix starts: 25   Grand Prix victories: 0 – best result: 3rd place, Austrian GP 1964
Points total: 8

An accomplished driver who regularly performed well beyond expectations.

Bob Anderson had enjoyed a successful career in motorcycling in the 1950s before injury made him turn his thoughts towards four wheels. He was almost 30 when he entered Formula Junior in 1961, moving up to F1 two years later with DW Racing Enterprises. He mainly competed in non-championship races in the Lola Mk4, the car John Surtees and Roy Salvadori had raced the previous season with the Bowmaker team. There were two championship starts that year, though on both occasions Anderson finished seven laps behind the winner, Jim Clark.

Outperforming bigger names

1964 was comfortably Anderson's best year, when he competed in all the European rounds of the championship. In Austria he took advantage of a spate of retirements to finish 3rd. The team was still using the Climax V8 engine, but now had a Brabham chassis. Anderson was also in the points at Zandvoort and finished 7th in both the Monaco and British GPs. These were impressive results from a privateer on a shoestring budget, Anderson often outperforming bigger names with greater resources. He finished the season in 11th place.

His one trouble-free drive of 1965 came at Monaco, where he finished 9th. An accident during practice for the Nurburgring brought a premature end to his season. He returned for the 1966 campaign, his Brabham fitted with an outdated four-cylinder Climax engine in an attempt to be competitive in the new 3-litre formula introduced that year. Yet again he punched above his weight, the highlight coming at Monza, where he finished 6th.

Tragedy prompts safety review

Anderson opened his 1967 campaign with a fine 5th place from 10th on the grid – ahead of Brabham, who had taken pole. There were two more top ten finishes before Anderson crashed during practice at Silverstone. He was trapped in his car for half an hour with perforated lungs before help arrived. He was eventually removed to hospital in an old, poorly equipped vehicle but did not survive. The death of a fine driver who regularly performed well beyond expectations prompted the BRDC to introduce new emergency procedures.

1965 Monaco Grand Prix. Bob Anderson (number 9, Brabham BT11 Climax) leads Frank Gardner and Jo Siffert (both Brabham BT11 BRM).

Peter Arundell

Born 8 November 1933 (Ilford, Essex)
Grand Prix starts: 11   Grand Prix victories: 0 – best result: 3rd place, Monaco GP 1964, Dutch GP 1964
Points total: 12

A rising star, Arundell was prevented from building on his early success after a serious injury.

Peter Arundell was a rising star of British motor racing in the early 1960s, but his bright flame flickered all too briefly. He entered Formula Junior in 1960, where he came up against and occasionally got the better of Jim Clark, who would be his future Grand Prix teammate. Arundell won the 1962 British Formula Junior title in a works Lotus 22, scoring eighteen wins from 25 starts. He also won the Monaco Formula Junior race, making it back-to-back wins in that prestigious event.

1963 saw Arundell compete in some non-championship F1 races, particularly when Trevor Taylor – ahead of him in the Lotus pecking order – fell victim to a number of injuries. However, he concentrated most of his efforts on winning the British Formula Three title and didn't make his Grand Prix debut until the following year, when Taylor was dropped.

Great start to Grand Prix career

Arundell competed in four GP races in 1964. He finished 3rd in his first two starts, Monaco and Zandvoort, and was in the points again in the fourth round, France, where he finished 4th. It was an excellent start to his championship career, although naturally he was in Clark's shadow. Arundell was prevented from building on these early successes after a bad injury in a Formula Two race at Reims. He sustained multiple fractures when his car was hit at high speed by Richie Ginther, although the eleven points he'd already accumulated were enough to earn him 8th equal in the 1964 championship, sharing that placing with Jack Brabham.

Colin Chapman kept a berth open for Arundell for the 1966 season but he scored just one point – 6th place in the penultimate race, the US Grand Prix. He retired from top-level racing after the final round, Mexico, where he finished 7th.

Derek Bell

Born 31 October 1941 (Pinner, Middlesex)
Grand Prix starts: 9   Grand Prix victories: 0 – best result: 6th place, United States GP
Points total: 1

The F1 statistics fail to do justice to one of the most talented drivers of his generation.

Derek Bell was undoubtedly one of the most talented drivers of his generation, and with a career spanning more than three decades he also achieved remarkable longevity in top-level motor sport. Bell starred in the junior formulae and had a glittering career in sports cars – he was five times a winner at Le Mans. But when he was given an opportunity in Grand Prix racing, circumstances conspired to leave him with a record not commensurate with his ability.

Bell began his racing career in 1964 in a Lotus 7 and was soon competing in Formula Three. Initially his mentor was his enthusiastic stepfather, but Bell realised that in order to progress he needed help from someone with a racing pedigree and teamed up with Peter Westbury. The successful run continued in Formula Two, and Bell took the eye of Ferrari, for whom he made his Grand Prix debut at Monza, 1968. He failed to finish there, and in his only other start that season, Watkins Glen.

Pipped for Formula Two title

Ferrari scaled back their racing operation in 1969, and that year Bell had only a one-off drive for McLaren, at the British Grand Prix. His suspension failed after just five laps. In 1970 Bell focused most of his efforts on the F2 championship, narrowly losing the title race to Clay Regazzoni. His backer was Tom Wheatcroft, and at Spa he ran a Brabham for the Wheatcroft team. His only other Grand Prix was for Team Surtees at Watkins Glen, where he finally registered a point for 6th place.

Five Le Mans victories

There were two more indifferent Grand Prix appearances in 1971, which contrasted with an excellent victory in the sports car championship in the Gulf Porsche. He managed five Grands Prix for Tecno in 1972 but didn't make it to the finishing line

once. There were no F1 championship races for Bell in 1973, and a return to Team Surtees the following year continued the disappointing run at that level. He qualified for just one of the five races entered, the German Grand Prix, where he crossed the line five minutes behind race winner Regazzoni. This was to be his ninth and final GP start. The following year he won the first of his five Le Mans titles, partnered by Jacky Ickx in the Gulf. Bell was still competing in top-level sports car events in the 1990s, and while the record books reflect his considerable achievements in that domain, the F1 statistics fail to do justice to his talent.

Mark Blundell

Born 8 April 1966 (Barnet, Hertfordshire)
Grand Prix starts: 61   Grand Prix victories: 0 – best result: 3rd place, South African GP 1993, German GP 1993, Spanish GP 1994
Points total: 32

Making an impact on the Formula One élite.

By the age of seventeen Mark Blundell was already a seasoned campaigner in motocross. He moved to four wheels that year with Formula Ford, the beginning of a seven-year haul in which he worked his way up to join the Formula One élite. By 1988 Blundell had secured a works drive in Formula 3000, with Lola. After a promising start, that season turned to one of frustration and disappointment. A change of team the following year yielded no improvement, Blundell failing to make an impact with Middlebridge. But his fortunes were set to improve. Nissan signed him for their sports car team, where he impressed, and in 1990 he joined Williams as a test driver. Patrese and Boutsen were the men in possession that year, with Mansell returning to the Williams fold to replace Boutsen at the end of the season. Blundell thus accepted an offer to join Brabham, where he partnered Martin Brundle.

Victory at Le Mans

He made his F1 debut at the US Grand Prix, Phoenix, the curtain-raiser of the '91 season. He finished just twice in the first ten races; in the eleventh, Spa, he notched his first championship point by coming home 6th. That was his tally for the season, although the experienced Brundle fared little better, scoring just two points. Brabham's finances were in a parlous state and Blundell was dropped at the end of the year. It was back to test driving in 1992, with McLaren, but the highlight of the season was a victory at Le Mans, where he was partnered by Derek Warwick and Yannick Dalmas.

1993 saw Blundell reunited with Brundle, this time with Ligier. In the first outing of the new campaign, Kyalami, he drove magnificently to secure his first podium, finishing 3rd behind Prost and Senna. He was in the points again in the second round, Interlagos. There was another 3rd at Hockenheim, and on four occasions he finished just out of the points. Ten points put him 10th in the drivers' championship that year. But there had been a few accidents too, and Blundell found himself on the move again for 1994.

Blundell promoted after Mansell quits

His best return that year was 3rd place at Catalunya. Although he outscored teammate Ukyo Katayama, the latter was retained and Blundell joined McLaren. When Nigel Mansell famously struggled to fit into the MP4/10, Blundell was promoted, scoring on his first outing. Mansell quit after just two appearances, and Blundell was given the berth for the rest of the season. He ended the year just four points behind teammate Mika Hakkinen in the championship, but the arrival of David Coulthard in 1996 left him without an F1 drive and he headed off to Indy Cars, where he enjoyed considerable success.

Tony Brooks

Born 25 February 1932 (Dukinfield, Cheshire)
Grand Prix starts: 38   Grand Prix victories: 6 (1 shared)
Points total: 75

By 1956 Brooks had become one of racing's hottest properties.

Along with Stirling Moss, Tony Brooks ranks as one of the greatest drivers never to win the world championship. Of the 38 Grands Prix in which Brooks started he won six and finished in the top six on fourteen occasions. Those statistics look even more impressive when the number of retirements is taken into consideration. Brooks failed to finish in seventeen of those races; thus, when his car did go the distance Brooks' success rate was better than one in four.

Breaks 30-year-old record

1955 was Brooks' breakthrough season. After moving to single-seaters he drove a Connaught to 4th place in the Daily Telegraph Trophy at Aintree behind three established F1 drivers. He then made a spectacular F1 debut, winning the non-championship Syracuse GP. It was the first time in over 30 years that a British car and driver had won on the Continent.

Brooks was suddenly one of motor racing's hottest properties. He signed for BRM for 1956, but it did not prove to be a productive season and he spent the next two years with Vanwall.

Shared victory in British GP

In 1957 he was partnered by Moss, and the two shared victory in the British Grand Prix. Moss's car failed and Brooks, carrying an injury sustained at Le Mans, handed over his car. He finished the season fifth in the championship, and also won the 1000km sports car race at the Nurburgring, beating both Fangio and Moss.

Constructors' title

1958 was Brooks' best year. He scored three GP victories – two more than the man who lifted the title – Mike Hawthorn – but six retirements in ten rounds cost him dear in a season when the best six scores decided the championship. There was consolation in the contribution he made towards

Vanwall taking the constructors' title.

Vanwall withdrew from racing at the end of 1958 and Brooks signed for Ferrari. There were two more victories – France and Germany – plus a 2nd in Monaco and 3rd in the US Grand Prix. It still wasn't quite enough: he finished four points behind champion Jack Brabham, who enjoyed the superior handling of the revolutionary rear-engined Cooper-Climax.

For 1960 Brooks joined the Yeoman Credit Racing Team. His old-style T51 Cooper was uncompetitive and his best showing was 4th in the Monaco GP. 1961 was his swansong season, for which he returned to BRM. The new 1.5-litre formula was not to his liking, and after finishing an excellent 3rd in the final round, 29-year-old Brooks retired to concentrate on his garage business.

Brooks with racing partner Stirling Moss in 1957.

Martin Brundle

Born 1 June 1959 (Kings Lynn, Norfolk)
Grand Prix starts: 158   Grand Prix victories: 0 – best result: 2nd place, Italian GP 1992, Monaco GP 1994
Points total: 98

Brundle's failure to register a single win remains one of the mysteries of Formula One.

In 1983 Martin Brundle notched seven wins in the British F3 Championship, narrowly losing the championship to Ayrton Senna. The fact that Senna went on to dominate F1 while Brundle failed to register a single win in twelve years remains one of the great mysteries of the sport.

In Brundle's first season at the top level, with Tyrrell, he finished 5th in Brazil and 2nd in Detroit, but had his points expunged after the team was found guilty of infringing regulations. The following two seasons yielded an aggregate of just eight points, and a year with the German Zakspeed team in 1987 was equally disappointing.

Victory in World Sports Car Championship
Apart from a one-off drive for Williams, 1988 saw Brundle focus on the World Sports Car Championship, which he won in a Jaguar. It was back to Grand Prix racing with Brabham in 1989, but once again it was a matter of wrong team, wrong time, as he garnered just four points from the campaign. He returned to sports cars in 1990, and then, after yet another uninspiring season with Brabham in '91, Brundle finally got the break he was looking for, signing for Benetton, alongside Michael Schumacher. A string of podiums made him competitive with all except Mansell in his title-winning season. Brundle ended the year stronger than Schumacher, scoring in each of the last nine races.

Signs for McLaren
Brundle signed for Ligier in '93. Third at Imola was his best result of the season, but Patrese – his replacement at Benetton – headed him by just seven points in the final table.

Senna's move to Williams for 1994 provided an opening at McLaren, and Brundle joined the team which had won the title seven times in ten years. But with Schumacher and Hill dominating for Benetton and Williams, Brundle was among the pack feeding off scraps. There were podiums at Monza and Hungary and three other points-scoring finishes, but Brundle failed to go the distance in nine races.

Brundle returned to Ligier in 1995,

sharing the number two spot with Aguri Suzuki. Brundle gave the team a podium finish at Spa, but it was hardly a satisfactory arrangement.

Brundle walks away from airborne crash
Brundle's final year in F1 was with Jordan. In the opening round, Melbourne, he was lucky to escape unhurt from a spectacular first-lap crash which sent his Jordan 196 into a barrel-roll. The car was uncompetitive and he scrapped for the minor placings, scoring in five rounds but never finishing higher than 4th.

The following year Brundle moved into the TV commentary box alongside Murray Walker. He had had a fine twelve-year career in F1, but surely would have achieved more had he joined teams at more propitious moments.

Jenson Button

Born 19 January 1980 (Frome, Somerset)
Grand Prix starts: 84*
Grand Prix victories: 0* - best result: 2nd place San Marino GP 2004, Monaco GP 2004, German GP 2004, Chinese GP 2004
Points total: 130*

*to end of 2004 season

The hottest young property in motor sport.

Jenson Button is widely regarded as the man most likely to become Britain's ninth world champion. He was a largely unknown quantity when he was catapulted into the F1 spotlight in 2000, aged just 20. Even so, he had a long pedigree in motor sport, having shone in the Cadet Kart class when he was just eight. He twice won the British championship in this division, went on to take a hat-trick of British Open titles, and was runner-up in the world championship. In 1997 17-year-old Button became the youngest ever European Formula Super A champion, and was emerging as motor sport's hottest young property.

Young Driver of the Year award

1998 saw Button move to Formula Ford with Haywood Racing. He stormed to the British title, picking up the McLaren-Autosport Young Driver of the Year award. It was on to F3 in 1999, and against much more experienced drivers he performed superbly to finish third in the championship. At the end of the year he tested for both McLaren and Prost, but it was Williams who snapped him up and gave him his first taste of F1.

Button finished 6th in only his second outing, Interlagos, becoming the youngest British driver in the championship's history to score a point. Several more superb performances, including 5th in his first home GP at Silverstone, gave Button twelve points and 8th

place in his debut season. Even so, for 2001 Williams turned to Montoya and Button departed to Benetton-Renault. Awaiting him there was a car still under development and it was no reflection on Button's talent that his only points came from a 5th place at Hockenheim.

Button outshines former world champion

Button's second season with Renault yielded seven top-six finishes as he outscored teammate Jarno Trulli and garnered fourteen points for 7th in the championship. However, Fernando Alonso was chosen to partner Trulli for 2003, and Button signed a two-year deal with BAR. Partnering Jacques Villeneuve, Button produced his best form to date and regularly outperformed the 1997 world champion. In 2004 Button scored ten podium finishes, 85 points putting him 3rd behind the Ferrari duo, Schumacher and Barrichello. He was instrumental in BAR finishing second in the constructors' title.

Button wanted to return to Williams for 2005, but the Contracts Recognition Board ruled that he was committed to BAR for another season. Fittipaldi and Schumacher were both 25 when they became world champion. If Button doesn't emulate that achievement in 2005, he still has the chance to become Britain's youngest ever champion, Jim Clark having been crowned when he was 27.

Jim Clark

4 March 1936 (Kilmany, Fife) - 7 April 1968
Grand Prix starts: 72   Grand Prix victories: 25   Points total: 274
World Champion 1963, 1965

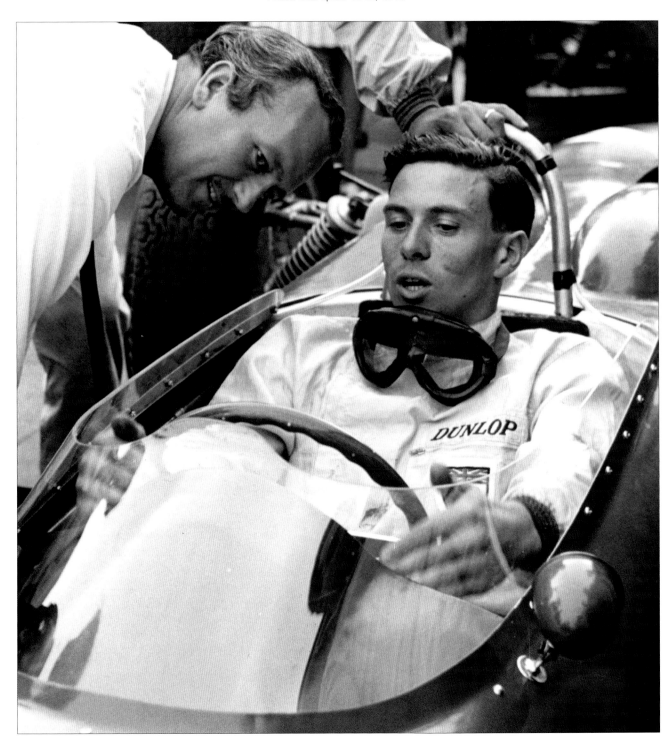

Unassuming off the track, Clark was formidable when he got behind the wheel.

Prost, Senna, Mansell and Stewart all sit higher than Jim Clark in the table of career F1 victories. But Clark's 25 wins came from just 72 starts, by some margin a better ratio than these other luminaries of the motor racing world.

Unassuming off the track, Clark was formidable when he got behind the wheel. Even as a child growing up on the family farm in the Scottish borders he would race his pedal-car at breakneck speed. After leaving school he did some rallying before competing in his first proper circuit race at a disused airfield near Aberdeen in 1956. He was soon winning regularly at such meetings, but while others saw star quality in the young Clark, waxing lyrical about his awesome speed and effortless control, he was initially diffident about his talent. Only much later did he recognise his gifts, and even when he made it to world number one he remained reserved, preferring the company of friends and family to the media spotlight.

Clark joins Lotus

Clark's first experience in a single-seater came in November 1958, when he tested at Brands Hatch in a Lotus F2 car. It was here that he first met Lotus boss Colin Chapman, an alliance which would prove so dominant in the 1960s. In 1959 Clark was asked to drive for Aston Martin, who were preparing to enter F1. The terms of the arrangement allowed Clark to drive for Lotus when Aston Martin wasn't competing. The deal fell through, enabling the Clark-Lotus partnership to take root.

Clark's first Grand Prix was at Zandvoort, where he took the place of John Surtees, then alternating between F1 and the 500cc championship.

Clark was undoubtedly the greatest driver of his era.

He had a terrific duel with Graham Hill and was running 5th before his gearbox failed. He garnered eight points from six races in 1960, including 3rd place in Portugal.

Car failure robs Clark of '62 title

There were two more podium finishes in 1961, but the season was marred by a collision with Wolfgang von Trips' Ferrari on the first lap at Monza. Fourteen spectators were killed and von Trips also lost his life.

Clark's first GP victory came at Spa, the third round of the 1962 championship. He also won at Aintree and Watkins Glen, but was most proud of his performance at the Nurburgring, run in atrocious conditions. After failing to start he carved his way through the field to finish 4th. He went into the final race, South Africa, trailing Graham Hill by nine points, but Clark's tally had come from four races, Hill's from five. With only the best five scores counting, Clark would have pipped Hill for the title with a victory at East London, as the latter only had 2nd places to discard. Clark took pole and stormed into the lead, only for the car to fail him at the three-quarter mark.

Championship won with maximum score

When Clark retired while leading in the first race of the 1963 championship, Monaco, it seemed as if the ill luck was set to continue. He then proceeded to win seven of the remaining nine races. As only the best six results counted, Clark had the luxury of discarding a first place and still finishing on a maximum 54 points, out of sight of Richie Ginther on 29. In the same season he picked up $100,000 for finishing second on his debut in the Indy 500, and could have gone one better had race winner Parnelli Jones been black-flagged for leaking oil. He put the record book straight by winning the event two years later.

Clark came close to defending his crown in 1964, despite a spate of mechanical problems. Needing to win the final race in Mexico he was leading with two laps to go before again hitting engine trouble.

Opposite: Clark with Colin Chapman and Lotus machanics.

Jim Clark and Graham Hill in the Reims
Formula 2 Grand Prix, Reims-Gueux, 1964.

Beats Fangio's record

In 1965 Clark finished six of the ten races, winning each time for another maximum 54-point haul and a second world title. Lotus didn't adapt well to the new 3-litre formula introduced for 1966, which proved to be a relatively lean season. In 1967 the new Lotus 49 with the Cosworth DFV engine made its debut. Clark won in it first time out, at Zandvoort, and scored three further victories to take 3rd in that year's championship behind the powerful Brabham-Repcos. It boded well for 1968,

and Clark took the opening round, Kyalami. It was his 25th victory, putting him ahead of Fangio in the all-time list. It was to be his last success. On 7 April he crashed in a Formula Two race at Hockenheim, killed instantly when his car went off the track and struck a tree.

Clark was a master on all circuits, in all conditions. He won two world titles, could easily have won on two other occasions, and was undoubtedly the greatest driver of his era.

Peter Collins

6 November 1931 (Kidderminster, Worcestershire) - 3 August 1958
Grand Prix starts: 32   Grand Prix victories: 3   Points total: 47

The sportsman who raced for the sheer love of the sport.

Peter Collins will always be remembered for an act of sportsmanship which cost him the chance of becoming world champion. Collins was still two months short of his 25th birthday when he handed his car over to Ferrari teammate Juan Manuel Fangio in the final round of the 1956 championship, allowing the Argentine to claim his fourth world crown. If the young Englishman thought time was on his side – Fangio was then 45 – he was mistaken, for two years later he was killed at the Nurburgring.

Collins was in the vanguard of British drivers who emerged in the postwar era. In 1948 he entered Formula 500 in a Cooper-Norton, where he spent three years. He made his world championship debut as a 20-year-old with HWM at the 1952 Swiss Grand Prix. One of his teammates that year was Stirling Moss. While Moss would go on to be regarded as one of the new breed of professional drivers, Collins raced for the sheer love of the sport. Neither driver made significant impact in 1952, however, the HWM sadly lacking in reliability.

Signs for Ferrari

Over the next three seasons Collins turned out for Vanwall and BRM as well as HWM, and also drove for Aston Martin's sports car team. His big break came in 1956 when he signed for Ferrari, although he was very much the talented understudy to the master, Fangio, who had also just joined from Mercedes. This was the era when drivers were able to share cars and split any points gained. In the second race, Monaco, Fangio took over Collins' Lancia Ferrari and steered it to 2nd place. Collins scored victories at Spa and Reims, and then finished second in the British Grand Prix. As championship leader at Silverstone it was Collins' turn to pull rank, taking over Alfonso de Portago's car to keep his title hopes on track.

Collins went into the final round, Monza, trailing Fangio by eight points; the championship could be his if he won and set the fastest

In an act of extraordinary magnanimity he offered Fangio his Ferrari.

lap, with his teammate failing to score. Fangio pitted on lap 18 with a steering problem. Luigi Musso, another Ferrari team member, had barely a championship point to his name yet he refused to hand Fangio his car.

'Because he deserved it'

Collins, by contrast, was running 3rd and had every chance of winning the ultimate prize when he came in for tyres at around the two-thirds distance. But in an act of extraordinary magnanimity he offered Fangio his Ferrari, which the Argentine steered to 2nd place. Fangio would never forget the part Collins played in his fourth championship victory, the Englishman finishing the title race in 3rd place. When asked why he had acted as he had, Collins replied simply: 'Because Fangio deserved it.'

Stylish victory over Hawthorn

Ferrari was off the pace in 1957 and two 3rd places represented Collins' best Grand Prix performances, although he did win two non-championship F1 races.

For 1958 the team fielded the new 246 Dino, with Collins, Hawthorn and Musso spearheading the challenge. After two top-six finishes Collins won the British Grand Prix in style from Hawthorn. Two weeks later, at the Nurburgring, he was chasing race leader Tony Brooks' Vanwall when he hit a bank and was thrown from his car. His death at 26 deeply affected Hawthorn and was a factor in the latter's decision to retire after winning that season's world crown. Collins finished posthumously equal 5th that year; 1956 thus remained his highest placing and, more importantly, the year in which top-level sport witnessed an act of extraordinary selflessness.

Opposite: Collins with Mike Hawthorn at the British Grand Prix

David Coulthard

Born 27 March 1971 (Twynholm, Kirkcudbrightshire)
Grand Prix starts: 175*   Grand Prix victories: 13*   Points total: 475*

*to end of 2004 season

The Formula One prodigy comes of age.

A junior karting champion, David Coulthard progressed to Formula Ford, winning the 1989 McLaren-Autosport Young Driver of the Year award. A year later he finished 4th in the Formula Vauxhall series. 1991 saw Coulthard finish runner-up in the British F3 championship, after which he spent two years in Formula 3000.

F1 opportunity follows Senna's death
Coulthard began 1994 still in F3000, although he was now also Williams' test driver. He was catapulted into the limelight after Senna's death at Imola. He contested eight races that year, including a fine 2nd in Estoril, enough to earn a seat for '95.

Coulthard was on the podium eight times in his first full campaign. A penalty for speeding in the pit lane cost him victory at Silverstone, and he also led at Monza before retiring. It all came right at Estoril, where he led virtually all the way. He took 3rd place in the championship, behind Schumacher and teammate Hill.

Joins McLaren
In 1996 Coulthard joined McLaren, initially a retrograde step as the MP4/11 could not compete with the FW18. His best result was 2nd in Monte Carlo, and he ended the campaign with just eighteen points.

McLaren was becoming increasingly competitive, and Coulthard won the '97 curtain-raiser, Melbourne, to give the team its first victory for four years. There was success at Monza too, and in the final race, at Jerez, he finished 2nd to teammate Mika Hakkinen for a McLaren one-two. Coulthard ended the season in equal 3rd place after Schumacher's points were expunged.

McLaren had the car to beat in both 1998 and 1999, but it was Hakkinen who cashed in. Coulthard's only victory in '98 came at Imola, although five 2nd places helped him to 3rd in the title race. There were two more wins in '99, Silverstone and Spa, but seven DNFs took their toll and Coulthard slipped to 4th in the championship.

Escapes unhurt from plane crash
The highlights of 2000 were another win at Silverstone and a first victory in Monaco.

However, his greatest stroke of luck that year was in walking away unscathed from a plane crash just after the British Grand Prix.

In 2001 he finally emerged from Hakkinen's shadow to carry the fight for McLaren, but it was only good enough for the runner-up spot – 58 points behind champion Schumacher.

Another win at Monaco was Coulthard's only success in 2002. He notched 41 points, over 100 less than Schumacher. In 2003 it was teammate Kimi Raikkonen who pushed Ferrari close, Coulthard slipping to 7th overall.

Coulthard's swansong year with McLaren was disappointing, but he did notch his 150th outing for the team, a record for a driver with one outfit. With 475 points to his name, Coulthard stood 6th in the all-time list, within ten points of overhauling both Mansell and Piquet.

Piers Courage

27 May 1942 (Colchester, Essex) - 21 June 1970
Grand Prix starts: 28   Grand Prix victories: 0 – best result: 2nd place, Monaco GP 1969, US GP 1969
Points total: 20

Both fast and erratic but racing was his passion.

Piers Courage was a member of the famous brewing family and heir to a considerable fortune, but from his days as an Eton schoolboy motor racing was his passion. Despite his wealthy connections Courage was given no assistance, save for the wherewithal to acquire a Lotus 7 at the start of his career; after that he was on his own. In the early 1960s Courage struggled to establish himself on the Formula Three circuit on a shoestring budget. In 1964 he formed Anglo-Swiss Racing with friend Jonathan Williams, competing in F3 races throughout Europe. There were a couple of encouraging podium finishes that year, and a string of victories over the following two seasons. These earned Courage a Formula Two start, at the 1966 German Grand Prix, where he crashed the Lotus of the Ron Harris works team.

Fast but erratic

Courage had two inauspicious championship outings for Reg Parnell Racing in 1967, but after spinning off at Monaco he found himself confined to another season in F2. There was no doubting his speed and thus potential to win races, but there were concerns that he was too erratic, and in particular that he was accident-prone.

Courage's racing credentials received a major boost with some stunning drives in the seven-race Tasman series early in 1968, where he ran a McLaren. Never lower than 5th going into the final race, he crowned the series with a spectacular victory, Jim Clark among those who were defeated on the day.

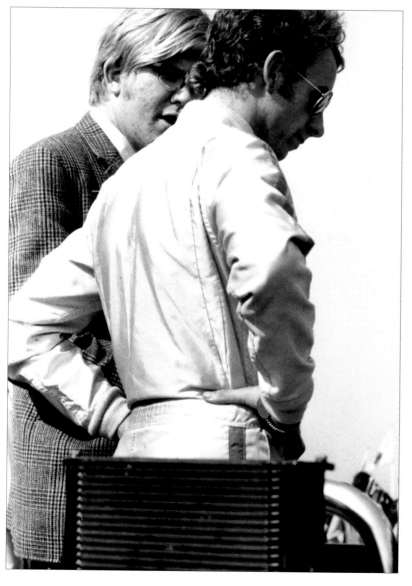

Courage joins forces with Williams

Courage contested virtually a full GP season in 1968, finishing 4th at Monza and getting in the points in France. He also competed in F2 for close friend Frank Williams, and when the latter entered F1 for the first time the following year with a Brabham, Courage was at the wheel. In only his 2nd outing, Monaco, he finished second, and repeated that achievement at the US GP. On both occasions he beat the works Brabhams of Ickx and the team boss himself. He also led briefly at Monza before suffering loss of fuel pressure and finishing 5th. An aggregate sixteen points put him 8th in the 1969 championship, a highly laudable effort.

For 1970 Williams opted to ditch the proven Brabham in favour of the Ford-powered de Tomaso, and Courage chose to stay despite a tempting offer from Ferrari. Early-season form was indifferent, but by the time the circus reached Holland in late June the teething problems with the car seemed to have been ironed out. But around quarter distance at Zandvoort Courage crashed and suffered fatal injuries when his car burst into flames.

Mike Hailwood

4 April 1940 (Great Milton, Oxfordshire) - 23 March 1981
Grand Prix starts: 50   Grand Prix victories: 0 – best result: 2nd place, Italian GP 1972
Points total: 29

The motorcycling legend awarded the George Medal for bravery.

Like John Surtees, Mike Hailwood was a legend in the world of motorcycling who tried to emulate that success on four wheels when there was nothing left to prove on two. Hailwood undoubtedly had the talent, and in different circumstances he might have added an F1 title to the nine world championships he accumulated on bikes.

Hailwood entered Formula Junior in 1963, and at Silverstone that year he drove a Lotus Climax to 8th place on his Grand Prix debut. That was for Reg Parnell Racing, for whom he also drove in the 1964 championship series. He was never out of the top ten when he finished, but five retirements made for a frustrating first full season. Hailwood again concentrated on bikes, while also enjoying considerable success in sports cars.

Closest Grand Prix finish ever

In 1971 he returned to Grand Prix racing with Team Surtees, for whom he had already won the F2 European championship. Monza saw Hailwood compete in his first Grand Prix for some six years, and he was involved in the closest finish of all time. Five cars crossed the line within 0.61 sec. of each other. Hailwood was 4th in that group – just 0.18 sec. behind the BRM of winner Peter Gethin – but it proved that he could compete with the very best.

Hailwood suffered a string of retirements in 1972, yet still finished in the points on four occasions. The highlight was Monza, where he finished 2nd to new world champion Emerson Fittipaldi. He might have gone one better at Kyalami, where he started fourth on the grid, set the fastest lap and was involved in a great battle for the lead before the suspension on his Surtees TS9B failed. Even so, he accumulated thirteen points to finish the season in 8th place.

Awarded George Medal

The Surtees car proved desperately unreliable in 1973. When it went the distance Hailwood invariably put it in the top ten, although he ended the season without a point to his name. He did distinguish himself at the South African GP when he rescued an unconscious Clay Regazzoni from his burning BRM after a pile-up on the third lap, an act of heroism for which he was awarded the George Medal, the highest civilian award for bravery.

Hailwood moved to McLaren in 1974, and had four top-six finishes under his belt when the circus moved to the Nurburgring, the eleventh round of the championship. He sustained severe leg injuries when he crashed out on lap 12; his F1 career was over.

Mike Hawthorn

10 April 1929 (Mexborough, Yorkshire) - 22 January 1959
Grand Prix starts: 45   Grand Prix victories: 3   Points total: 127.64
World Champion 1958

Dapper and flamboyant – the first Britain to capture the world crown.

Racing was in the blood of the dapper, flamboyant Mike Hawthorn, the man destined to become the first Briton to capture the world crown. Father Leslie had competed in TT races and ran a family garage business in Farnham, where the family moved when Mike was three.

In his youth Mike did some motorcycle scrambling before moving on to four-wheel speed trials in the late 1940s. He moved up to F2 – then world championship category – in 1952, beating the great Fangio in a Cooper-Bristol in April of that year at Goodwood. This brought instant celebrity, and with his shock of blond hair and engaging personality, Hawthorn was feted as one of motor sport's rising stars.

He finished 4th in his first Grand Prix, at Spa on 22 June 1952, and ended his debut championship campaign 4th equal in a season dominated by Ferrari.

Signs for Ferrari

Hawthorn's performances caught the eye of Enzo Ferrari himself, and he signed for the Italian giant for the 1953 season, winning his first Grand Prix at Reims on 5 July. He pipped Fangio in a daring outbraking manoeuvre on the last corner, after which the Argentine magnanimously paid tribute to the new British ace. Hawthorn picked up points in each race and again finished the championship in 4th place.

His second season with Ferrari was blighted by a bad accident in the non-championship Syracuse GP, and there was also a furore over his failure to undertake National Service, the matter reaching the floor of the House of Commons. In fact he suffered from a serious kidney complaint which would have debarred him from military service, though typically he never made an issue of a condition that would eventually cause him to

Hawthorn, the born racer, clinches the world crown by a single point.

suffer blackouts. He won the final race of the 1954 season, the Spanish GP, to claim 3rd place in that year's championship.

Criticism follows worst ever accident

In 1955 Hawthorn had an unhappy spell in an uncompetitive Vanwall. He did win at Le Mans in a Jaguar that year but the victory was marred by motor racing's worst ever accident. Hawthorn was involved in the incident, which resulted in 82 deaths and came in for criticism from some commentators.

After two lean GP seasons, including a disappointing spell with BRM, Hawthorn finished 4th in the 1957 championship, by now reunited with Ferrari. The following year, his seventh campaign, it finally all came right. He won only one race, the French GP, but was consistently in the points. He clinched the title by a single point after finishing 2nd to his closest rival, Stirling Moss, in the final round at Morocco.

Devastated by death of Collins

Shattered by the death of his teammate and close friend Peter Collins – killed at that year's German GP – and debilitated by the worsening kidney condition, Hawthorn announced his retirement in December that year. Just a few weeks later, 22 January 1959, he was killed after losing control of his Jaguar on Guildford bypass on the way to a meeting. With his dashing good looks, ultra-competitive spirit and an essentially amateur mentality for the sport he loved, Hawthorn gained a special place in the affection of the fans, and gave Britain her first taste of success in motor racing's premier competition.

Opposite: Tony Brooks and Mike Hawthorn explain their late race retirements at Spa in 1958.

Johnny Herbert

Born 25 June 1964 (Brentwood, Essex)
Grand Prix starts: 145   Grand Prix victories: 3   Points total: 98

One of Britain's most exciting young talents of the 1980s.

Johnny Herbert was one of Britain's most exciting young talents of the 1980s, tipped by many to go right to the top. A former British karting champion, Herbert moved up to Formula Ford in 1983. He won the 1985 Formula Ford Festival at Brands Hatch, and a year later was on the podium in Formula Three. He took the eye of Eddie Jordan, who signed him for the 1987 F3 season. That was a championship-winning campaign, and for 1988 both Herbert and Jordan entered F3000. He won first time out and was on course to win the title when, on 21 August, a shunt at Brands Hatch left him with appalling foot injuries. Herbert was sidelined for six months, though track debris was still working its way out of his body years later.

Stunning F1 debut

Herbert signed for Benetton, making a stunning F1 debut in Brazil, where he finished 4th. It was clear that he hadn't fully recovered from his injuries, however, and he spent much of 1990 in Japan, competing in sports cars and the F3000 championship.

In late 1990 he received a call from Lotus, who had just lost Martin Donnelly through injury. Herbert ended the F1 season for the team, and stayed on for three more years. Unfortunately, Lotus was in decline, and Herbert's best return came in 1993: eleven points and 9th place in the championship. His best performance of this period came in 1991, when he won at Le Mans.

Victory at Silverstone

Lotus went into administration in 1994, and Herbert returned to Benetton. He won his first GP on home soil at Silverstone, and took the chequered flag at Monza to finish 4th in the championship. Unfortunately, he was inevitably in the shadow of teammate and champion Michael Schumacher.

Herbert moved to Sauber in 1996, and at Monaco gave the team its first podium. The car was not competitive, however, and hopes of a big improvement with the arrival of the new Petronas engine for '97 were soon dashed. Third place in Hungary was Herbert's

best showing, and he just squeezed into the top ten in the championship table.

Herbert gives Stewart-Ford maiden success

Jean Alesi joined the team in 1998, and although Herbert finished in the points in the curtain-raiser, Australia, the Frenchman got more out of the car and took over as number one. Herbert departed for the Stewart-Ford team, but there was more frustration as he suffered a string of DNFs in the early part of the 1999 season. He scored his first points for the team in Canada, then won at the Nurburgring. 2000 was a hugely disappointing year, however. The car didn't handle well, and long before the campaign was over Herbert announced his retirement from F1.

Damon Hill

Born 17 September 1960 (London)
Grand Prix starts: 116   Grand Prix victories: 22   Points total: 360
World Champion 1996

Damon exploited his advantage to the full to take his place alongside Graham in the sport's hall of fame.

As the son of a double world champion the spotlight on Damon Hill was always more intense, the level of expectation so much higher than with other fledgling racing drivers. He was determined to emulate his father's success, and the road to his 1996 world title was long and not always smooth. He had the good fortune of being in the right car at the right time in his glory year, but exploited the advantage to the full to take his place alongside Graham in the sport's hall of fame.

As a teenager Hill was keener on bikes than cars, and it was on two wheels that he made his first forays into competitive motor sport. He tried Formula Ford 2000 in 1983 but struggled to make the transition, the glare of media scrutiny not helping his cause. He stepped down to Formula Ford 1600 in 1984, combining this with a much more successful season on his 350cc Yamaha. He won five Formula Ford races in 1985, and the following year contested the British F3 championship. Progress was steady rather than spectacular: 9th in that year's championship, peaking at 3rd in his third year in F3, 1988.

Testing for Williams

It was on to F3000 next, and another three years spent learning his trade and earning every step up the ladder. The second of those, with Middlebridge, saw Hill regularly front-running but he failed to convert any of these opportunities into victories. His third F3000 campaign was with Eddie Jordan Racing, but his Lola was not the best in the division and he finished the series in 7th place. He did land a testing contract with Williams, though it was Brabham who gave him his first taste of F1. Hill's baptism at the top level in 1992 was a fiery one. He qualified the Judd-engined Brabham just twice, at Silverstone and the Hungaroring. In both races he finished four laps down on the race winner.

Maiden victory in Hungary

Fortunately for Hill, he had impressed Williams enough during testing for them to ignore his torrid time with Brabham and offer him a drive for 1993. He quickly began repaying the team's faith in him. He had spells in the lead in seven of the first ten races but, agonisingly, these yielded four 2nd places. Barcelona and Silverstone were particularly galling as the engine on Hill's Williams blew when he was in a strong position.

In Germany he suffered a puncture two laps from the line. He finally grabbed his maiden victory in Hungary, leading from start to finish from second on the grid after pole man, teammate Alain Prost, stalled on the parade lap and had to start from the back. Two races later Hill had turned that into a hat-trick of wins, and he ended his first full season 3rd behind Prost and Senna.

Hill number one after Senna's death

Having been junior partner to Prost, Hill then found himself partnering the other biggest name in F1, Ayrton Senna. But after Senna's death at Imola in 1994, Hill was suddenly team leader. He rose to the challenge in fine style. Victory at Catalunya began an eleven-race run in which he won six races and finished out of the top two only once. Going into the final race, Adelaide, Hill trailed Michael Schumacher by one point. It had been a controversial year for the German, who had been handed a two-race ban for ignoring a black flag at

Hill led all the way to take the crown by nineteen points.

Silverstone, then disqualified at Spa for a technical infringement on his Benetton. The showdown produced more controversy as Schumacher hit a wall and, knowing his race was over, took out Hill to seal the championship by that single point.

It was runner-up to Schumacher again in 1995. Both Williams and Benetton had the same Renault unit, and the German undoubtedly had the edge. There were four more wins for Hill, but with all scores counting, his failure to register in seven races proved critical and he finished the year 33 points adrift of the defending champion. The cars of the big two had clashed on three more occasions during the year, setting up another mouthwatering head-to-head in 1996.

Challenge from Villeneuve

Everything augured well for the new campaign. Schumacher had moved to Ferrari and would inevitably need time to adjust; and with Coulthard leaving Williams, Hill now had rookie Jacques Villeneuve as a partner. With four wins in the first five races it seemed that he was going to canter to the winning post. But it quickly became clear that the major threat would come from his teammate, who brought the form that had made him Indycar champion into F1. Even with seven wins under his belt, Hill had to score in the final race, Suzuka, to be sure of the title. In the end it was academic. Villeneuve failed to finish, while Hill led all the way to take the crown by nineteen points.

Replaced by Frentzen

Even before the championship was sealed it was confirmed that Hill was to be replaced by Sauber's Heinz-Harald Frentzen. With no top ride available, Hill joined Arrows in 1997. It was a very different story for the

Opposite: Damon Hill (Williams FW18 Renault) leads at the start into Curva do Sol Brazilian Grand Prix, Interlagos, Brazil. March 1996.

reigning champion, who got into the points in just two outings. Hungary was the highlight. He was leading on the last lap, only for his car to splutter, creating a welcome opportunity for Villeneuve; Hill limped home second behind his former teammate.

Hill's final two seasons in F1 were spent with Jordan. The first half of 1998 was undistinguished, the car not yet properly developed. But he scored in five of the last six races, including his 22nd and final career

win, in the wet at Spa. Hill thus answered his critics, who maintained it was the Williams FW18 that had won the world crown. He also had the immense satisfaction of handing Jordan its first victory.

1999 was an anticlimax, Hill notching just seven points all year. With nothing left to prove, he walked away from a sport he had graced for almost two decades.

Graham Hill

15 February 1929 (London) - 29 November 1975
Grand Prix starts: 176   Grand Prix victories: 14   Points total: 289
World Champion 1962, 1968

Through sheer dedication and commitment he honed his skills to reach the very top of his profession.

The public face of Graham Hill was jocular, witty, urbane, a darling of the media who rubbed shoulders with royalty. With his clipped moustache, swept-back hair and jutting jaw Hill cut a dashing figure, comfortably assuming the unofficial role of motor sport's ambassador in the 1960s. In private he was very different: ruthless and driven, a man with grit and determination who was passionate about motor racing and intolerant of anyone who gave less than their best. By common consent he was not in the first rank of gifted drivers in terms of natural ability. But through sheer dedication and commitment he honed his skills to reach the very top of his profession.

Hill had little contact with cars before the age of 24, when he became the proud owner of a Morris 8, driving it home without first having taken the trouble to pass his test. In 1953 he responded to an advertisement offering anyone the chance to drive an F3 car round Brands Hatch at five shillings a lap. Four laps and one pound later Hill knew that this was where his future lay, and from that moment he lived and breathed motor racing.

Graham, Damon and Samantha Hill
at the Italian Grand Prix, 1967.

49

The first man to win the 24 Hour race, the Indy 500 and the world championship.

F1 debut at Monaco

Hill was a qualified engineer and worked for Colin Chapman at Lotus in the mid-1950s, racing Lotus Climaxes and Lotus Fords while waiting to break into Formula One. That came in 1958 at Monaco, the circuit with which his name would become synonymous. He was running 4th in his front-engined Lotus 16 but failed to finish, something which would become a recurring theme over the next two years. In frustration he joined BRM in 1960, and although he garnered just four points in his first season, by late 1961 the team had developed a V8 car capable of making a serious bid for the championship.

Hill won the opening round of the 1962 series, at Zandvoort, the first of his fourteen career victories and BRM's first success for three years. He took the flag at the Nurburgring and Monza too, and also registered two 2nd places, finishing behind Jim Clark in Belgium and the US. Hill went into the final round, the South African GP, with a nine-point advantage over Clark, but knowing that if the Scot won at East London they would each have 39 points from their best five races. Clark would then take the title by dint of having won four races to Hill's three. It was all academic, as Clark's Lotus gave out at the three-quarter distance and Hill took both the race and the world crown.

Ferrari team tactics rob Hill

Hill finished runner-up in each of the next three championship campaigns. Clark got his revenge in 1963 and 1965, winning by some distance, but in 1964 Hill agonisingly lost out to John Surtees. He went into the final round, Mexico City, leading the Ferrari driver by five points. With Hill out of contention, Surtees was ushered into 2nd place by teammate Lorenzo Bandini, giving him the six points he needed to snatch the title. In these three seasons Hill had the consolation of adding six more victories to his tally, winning both the US and Monaco Grands Prix each year.

Opposite the 1963 Silverstone International Trophy. Top to bottom: Jack Brabham, Bruce McLaren, Graham Hill, Innes Ireland.

In 1966 Hill won the Indianapolis 500 in a Lola-Ford, then rejoined Lotus, where he teamed up with Clark. 1967 was a disappointment but the new Lotus 49 promised great things for 1968. After Clark's death early in the season Hill restored morale in the Lotus camp, scoring three victories on the way to a second world title.

Horrific crash at Watkins Glen
In 1969 Hill notched his fifth Monaco success but suffered horrific injuries after crashing at Watkins Glen. He was back in the driving seat just five months later,

for the start of the 1970 series, but never challenged for top honours again. He did win Le Mans for Matra in 1972, however, securing a place in the record books as the first man to win the 24 Hour race, the Indy 500 and the world championship. He retired in 1975 to concentrate on establishing his own team. On 29 November Hill was piloting his light aircraft as the fledgling team returned to Elstree from testing at Paul Ricard. The plane struck a tree, killing Hill and five crew members, including young driving protégé Tony Brise.

James Hunt

29 August 1947 (Belmont, Surrey) - 15 June 1993
Grand Prix starts: 92   Grand Prix victories: 10   Points total: 179
World Champion 1976

Hunt had a steely, ultra-competitive quality which carried him all the way to the top.

James Hunt was a public schoolboy who eschewed a professional career path in favour of a life in racing, a decision which meant a hand-to-mouth existence for several years. A flamboyant, laid-back extrovert, Hunt also had a steely, ultra-competitive quality which carried him all the way to the top.

Hunt did a variety of menial jobs to fund his first sortie into racing, in a Mini. He then bought a Formula Ford on hire purchase, and in 1969 it was on to Formula Three. The early 1970s saw Hunt involved in a spate of accidents, which almost inevitably led to the sobriquet 'Hunt the Shunt'.

In 1972 he was driving a works March in the F3 championship, but quit the team after a row. Serendipity then took a hand. Lord Hesketh and Anthony 'Bubbles' Horsley were running a Formula Three team, and when the latter decided that his driving days were over, the two parties fell into each other's arms.

Hesketh steps up to F1

For 1973 Hesketh decided to mount a serious challenge by swapping the outdated March for the proven Surtees-Hart. The decision backfired somewhat, but after Hunt finished 3rd in the non-championship Race of Champions at Brands Hatch, Hesketh opted to put all his eggs in the F1 basket. An F1 March was procured on a hire basis, and Hunt qualified for his first Grand Prix, Monaco. He was running 6th when his engine gave out, finishing 9th. In his next outing, the French GP, Hunt earned his first point with a 6th-place finish. He followed this up with 4th at Silverstone after a restart, and then a first appearance on the podium for 3rd at Zandvoort. In the final race, Watkins Glen, Hunt crossed the line barely half a second behind the Lotus of Ronnie Peterson in a race from which new champion Jackie

Stewart withdrew following the death of his Tyrell teammate François Cevert. Fourteen points and 8th place – a better return than Ickx in the Ferrari – meant that F1 had to take the Hesketh outfit seriously, irrespective of the shoestring budget on which it was operating.

Maiden victory amid financial crisis

For 1974 the team decided to run its own car. The Ford-powered Hesketh 308 made its debut in South Africa, proving to be quick but unreliable. Hunt finished only six races, getting in the points in four of those. It was 8th place in the championship again, and just one point more from a full season, a frustrating return.

Improvements were made to the car for 1975, but the team was struggling financially. Sponsors stayed away, feeling that the quirky character of the outfit was too idiosyncratic. Hunt scored his maiden victory at

Hunt's dramatic title showdown with Lauda in Fuji.

Zandvoort, and finished the season strongly to claim 4th place in the title race, albeit over 30 points adrift of champion Niki Lauda.

Hesketh withdrew at the end of the year. Emerson Fittipaldi's decision to leave McLaren created an opening, and with Lauda ensconced at Ferrari, Hunt was the obvious choice.

Lauda opens up big lead

The move came so late that Hunt was still introducing himself to the McLaren M23 when he put it on pole at Interlagos, the 1976 curtain-raiser. He was running second to Lauda when he retired. It was another pole at Kyalami, and this time he finished 2nd, but Lauda made it successive victories. After crashing out at Long Beach, Hunt won in Spain, but Lauda picked up another six points for 2nd place. The McLaren was found to have infringed the new regulations regarding car dimensions and Hunt was disqualified. While this went to appeal, the racing continued. Hunt missed out at Zolder and Monaco, and Lauda stretched his lead by winning both. France brought a triple bonus for Hunt. He won the race, Lauda retired, and the points from Jarama were reinstated. Even so, Hunt trailed Lauda by 26 points.

A pile-up meant a restart at Brands Hatch. Hunt won, but Ferrari protested that he should have been excluded from the restart as he wasn't running when the first race was stopped. Again it went to appeal. Hunt was in sparkling form at the Nurburgring, while Lauda suffered life-threatening injuries in a fireball accident. Incredibly, Lauda missed just two races, in which Hunt finished 4th and 1st. The two met again at Monza, Hunt spinning off while Lauda came home 4th. It was now 61-56 in the Austrian's favour, but the FIA upheld Ferrari's protest from the British GP. Hunt's nine points were lost, while Lauda gained three. The gap was now 64-47.

Title showdown at Fuji

Hunt needed victories, and in Canada and the United States he got them. Going into the final race, Fuji, Hunt was three points behind the reigning champion. Conditions were atrocious

and Lauda quickly decided that he wasn't prepared to risk his neck. Hunt's tyres were shredded with the laps running out. He pitted for new wets, unsure where he stood in the race standings. In fact he was 5th, and in a furious late charge he overtook Regazzoni and Jones to gain the 3rd place he needed to clinch the title.

Hunt won three races for McLaren in 1977 but the team went into slow decline and Hunt's motivation and interest waned. 1978 was a disaster, and a move to Wolf the following year proved no better and he quit mid-season.

In the 1980s Hunt carved out a highly successful career as a TV commentator. He was in his usual place alongside Murray Walker for the Canadian GP, Montreal, on 13 June 1993. Two days later the 45-year-old died from a massive heart attack.

Above: 1976 British Grand Prix, Brands Hatch. James Hunt (McLaren Ford) won but was later disqualified for using the spare car in the restart.
Opposite: Hunt with Barry Sheene (seated) at the 1976 Japanese Grand Prix, Mount Fuji.

Eddie Irvine

Born 10 November 1965 (Newtownards, Co. Down)
Grand Prix starts: 146   Grand Prix victories: 4   Points total: 191

A spectacular debut as the Ulsterman forces the pace.

This brash Ulsterman made his name in Formula Ford, taking the British title in 1987 and winning the Formula Ford Festival at Brands Hatch in the same year. It was on to F3 in 1988, and F3000 a year later. He finished 3rd in the 1990 championship, and set his sights on a Formula One drive. This he achieved in 1993, for Jordan. It was a spectacular debut, taking a point for finishing 6th and also a punch from race winner Senna, who took exception when the lapped Irvine re-passed him. The pugnacious Irvine commented that Senna had been going too slowly.

Banned after shunt at Interlagos

1994 also began controversially as Irvine received a one-race ban for his part in a shunt at Interlagos. 4th at Jerez was his best performance of the season. Irvine remained with Jordan in 1995, and although his performances did not always translate into points, he regularly outpaced teammate Rubens Barrichello. He got on the podium for the first time in Canada, where he finished 3rd, but seven retirements hampered progress.

Supporting role

In 1996 Irvine got his big break, a move to Ferrari, alongside Michael Schumacher. 1997 saw him take 2nd in Argentina and four more podiums en route to 7th in the championship, but he was obviously playing second fiddle to Schumacher. In the penultimate round, Suzuka, Irvine played the supporting role to perfection, allowing Schumacher to take the lead from him and blocking rival Villeneuve. Irvine's work was undone when Schumacher had all his points expunged for a reckless manoeuvre in the showdown at Jerez.

It was more of the same in 1998. Irvine had his best season to date – 47 points and 4th in the championship – but he was a long way off the pace of his Ferrari teammate.

No. 1 at Ferrari after Schumacher injury

1999 was the year in which Irvine nearly made it to the top. Injury to Schumacher meant that Irvine became the focus of Maranello attention. He won three races, including the

inaugural Sepang GP. Here, in the penultimate race, it was the returning Schumacher who helped secure an Irvine victory. The Ulsterman went into the final round two points adrift of reigning champion Hakkinen. He was unable to bridge that gap and had to settle for the runner-up spot.

Irvine left Ferrari to head Jaguar's assault on F1 in 2000. The following three years were beset by difficulties, both with the cars and behind the scenes. Irvine accumulated just eighteen points in three seasons, although he did give the team its first podium, finishing 3rd in the 2001 Monaco GP. In 2002 a frustrated Irvine took 3rd at Monza and scored all eight of the team's points that season but his contract was not renewed.

Nigel Mansell

Born 8 August 1953 (Upton-on Severn, Worcestershire)
Grand Prix starts: 187   Grand Prix victories: 31   Points total: 482
World Champion 1992

Mansell roars into the Formula One list of all time greats.

A glance at the all-time F1 records shows the huge contribution Nigel Mansell made to the sport. In the top ten for number of Grands Prix contested; fifth highest points scorer; fourth in terms of championship race victories; 32 poles puts him 5th in that list; and he set the fastest race lap on 30 occasions, only Schumacher and Prost beating that mark.

Mansell enjoyed considerable success in karting before moving on to Formula Ford, in which he became British champion in 1977. He went into debt to fund a foray into F3 the following year, and by 1980 he had secured a Formula Two drive with Honda. Colin Chapman recognised his potential and took him as test driver at Lotus, for whom he made his Grand Prix debut at the Austrian GP in 1980. He failed to finish any of the three races he contested towards the end of that championship series, but a full campaign for Lotus the following year brought more encouraging results. He scored in three races, 3rd at Zolder being the highlight.

Move to Williams
brings dramatic improvement

Three more seasons with Lotus showed steady improvement but still there was no victory. The closest he came to a maiden win was Monaco '84, where he qualified 2nd and was leading at the halfway mark of a truncated race before crashing out. That year saw him break into the top ten for the first time, finishing the championship on thirteen points, equal with a certain Ayrton Senna in 9th place.

1985 saw Mansell join Williams, the beginning of a long and successful partnership spread over two stints. The improvement was dramatic. He scored back-to-

back victories at the European GP – staged at Brands Hatch – and Kyalami, helping him to a 31-point haul and 6th place in the title race. Williams teammate Keke Rosberg, the 1982 champion, notched just nine more points.

Blow-out costs Mansell title

In both of the next two seasons it was a case of 'so near, so far'. In 1986 Nelson Piquet joined Mansell and the pair virtually matched each other point for point, something from which McLaren's Prost would ultimately profit. Round two, Jerez, saw Mansell finish

It all finally came right in 1992. The FW14B and Nigel Mansell were all but invincible.

0.014 sec. behind Senna after 188 miles of racing, the third closest finish of all time. Mansell punched the air, believing he'd won, but the finishing line had been moved; had it remained in its original position the Englishman would have won a famous victory. Even so, there were five wins, which put Mansell on the threshold of the title when the circus went to Adelaide for the final round. He held a six-point advantage over Prost, but a blown tyre at the three-quarter distance cost him the championship, the Frenchman taking the chequered flag to snatch the crown by two points.

Six victories not quite enough

It was runner-up again in 1987, this time at the hands of Piquet. There was little love lost between the two, and with no team orders they were left to battle it out on the track. Mansell had already won twice when they came to Silverstone. Piquet took pole and led for 62 of the 65 laps. Mansell was almost 30 seconds off the pace at one stage but reeled his teammate in with a virtuoso performance. A stunning passing manoeuvre two laps from home sent home fans delirious. Mansell scored six victories to Piquet's three, but a crash during qualifying for Suzuka, the penultimate race, put paid to his chances.

1988 was a disappointment, Williams suffering badly after losing the tried and tested Honda engine and having to field an uncompetitive Judd V8 unit. Mansell then signed for Ferrari, where he spent two years. He opened his account for Maranello with a victory in the 1989 curtain-raiser, Interlagos, but McLaren dominated the season. Mansell's tally of 38 points, giving him 4th place, was only half that of the champion, Prost.

Runner-up for the third time

The Frenchman joined Mansell at Ferrari in 1990, and the latter notched just one victory as Prost and Senna resumed their great rivalry, streets ahead of the field. Mansell believed Prost was being favoured and flirted with the idea of retirement, but was persuaded by Williams to return to the fold. The FW14 once again had

formidable engine power, courtesy of Renault, and Mansell added five more wins to his tally. It only gave him the runner-up spot yet again – this time to Senna – and it could have been better had his car not failed within sight of victory in Montreal: he'd led for 68 of the 69 laps but in the end limped home 6th. There was also a disqualification at Estoril, for infringing pit regulations, in a race he had led for ten laps.

Mansell and FW14B invincible

It all finally came right in 1992. The FW14B, with its Renault V10 engine and active suspension, was all but invincible. Mansell put the car on pole in all but two races, took nine wins from the sixteen-race series and wrapped up the title with five rounds still to go. He finished the campaign on 108 points, 52 more than his Williams teammate Riccardo Patrese.

Mansell announced his retirement long before the end of his title-winning season. He was unhappy that Prost was on his way to Williams, and about contractual terms he saw as ill-befitting a man who had done so much for the team in his two spells there.

Rookie victory in Indycars

In 1993 Mansell moved to Indycars and promptly won that title too, winning five races. His second season was not so successful and he made a dramatic return to F1 with Williams, who had lost new signing Senna in the fatal accident at Imola. His fourth outing, the final race of the season at Adelaide, brought Mansell his 31st and final victory. He signed off from the sport he had graced in 1995 with a move to McLaren. Initially he couldn't fit into the car's cockpit, and Mark Blundell was drafted in to cover for the first two races. After just two appearances Mansell quit, an inauspicious end to an F1 career littered with glittering achievements.

Stirling Moss

Born 17 September 1929 (London)
Grand Prix starts: 66   Grand Prix victories: 16 (1 shared)
Points total: 186.64

When Fangio departed the scene in 1958 Moss was widely regarded as the finest driver in the world.

The name Stirling Moss became synonymous with British motor racing in the 1950s. When Fangio departed the scene in 1958 Moss was widely regarded as the finest driver in the world. Between 1955 and 1961 he never finished out of the top three, and on four occasions had to settle for the runner-up spot in the championship. Although he failed to capture the world title – agonisingly so in 1958 – this in no way detracts from a glorious career peppered with memorable achievements.

Moss began his competitive career in hill climbs in the late 1940s before moving on to Formula 500.

This category – which evolved into Formula Three – made top-level motor racing more affordable and less élitist, and Moss was at the forefront of the crop of talented young British drivers to emerge during this period.

Eye-catching performances
Moss's Grand Prix debut came with HWM in the Swiss GP, 1951, where he finished 8th. He came 2nd in the 1952 Monte Carlo Rally and entered numerous sports car races en route to securing a berth in a competitive F1 car. During this period Moss drove for both ERA and

Stirling Moss (F2 HWM-Alta) leading in the 1951 Lavant Cup 2000cc voiturette race at Goodwood.

Moss's place among the sport's legendary names was secured long before his enforced retirement.

Connaught, but these were well off the pace compared with the dominant marques of the day, Ferrari and Maserati.

In the 1953 German Grand Prix he drove a Cooper T23 to a fine 6th place, the only non-Italian car in the top eight. Performances such as this caught the eye of the major teams, and Moss enhanced his reputation still further when he ran his own Maserati in 1954. A superb 3rd place at Spa convinced Maserati, who promptly offered him a works drive. He led for 20 laps at Monza and had victory almost within his grasp when his oil tank ruptured. He pushed it over the line to finish 10th, showing all the determination of the new breed of professionals.

Maiden victory at Aintree

Mercedes snapped Moss up for 1955, and with Fangio alongside him the team dominated in the formidable Silver Arrows. Fangio was still the master, though Moss took the flag at the British GP at Aintree for his maiden victory.

Mercedes withdrew from racing in the wake of that year's Le Mans tragedy, and Moss rejoined Maserati, who were still running the excellent 250F. Two more victories helped Moss to the runner-up spot again, this time just three points behind Fangio in the final table.

The next two seasons, both with Vanwall, yielded six more wins. In 1957 he made it a hat-trick of 2nd places, all to Fangio. In 1958 he won four Grands Prix, yet lost out by a single point to Hawthorn, who crossed the line first just once. He showed great sportsmanship after the race in Portugal, where his evidence helped exonerate championship rival Hawthorn, who had been accused of infringing the regulations by pushing his car on the track. Hawthorn took 2nd place behind Moss, securing valuable

Above: Stirling Moss (Vanwall) makes his last pitstop at the British Grand Prix, Aintree, 1957. He finished in 1st position with Tony Brooks. This was the first victory in a World Championship Grand Prix for a British car.
Opposite: Moss (Lotus 18/21-Climax) crosses the line to win the German Grand Prix at Nurburgring, 6 August 1961.

points. In the showdown race – Morocco – Moss had to win, set the fastest lap and hope Hawthorn finished no better than 3rd. He did his part, but Hawthorn was allowed through to 2nd by his Ferrari teammate Phil Hill.

Costly mechanical failure

Moss had had a one-off drive for Cooper at the start of the 1958 season, winning in Argentina to give that marque its first success. When Vanwall withdrew from racing he joined Rob Walker's privateer outfit for 1959, competing mainly in a Cooper T51. He went into the final round, the first ever US Grand Prix, with yet another chance of winning the coveted title. But after taking pole and leading for five laps his car succumbed to gearbox trouble and he finished the title race in 3rd place.

Spectacular crash at Spa

For 1960 the Walker team fielded a Lotus 18 and at Monaco Moss gave Colin Chapman's car its first

victory. The following month he was thrown from his car after losing a wheel during practice for Spa. He sustained a serious back injury which put him out of racing for the the next four rounds. He returned in time to win the championship finale, the US GP, securing a fine 3rd place overall in a blighted season.

In 1961 Moss found himself up against the dominant Ferrari 156, yet still pulled off two spectacular victories in his underpowered Lotus. Victories in Monaco and Germany that year rank among his finest drives, considering the inferior hardware he was running.

The curtain on a glorious career came down early in 1962, when he suffered head injuries after crashing out in a non-championship race at Goodwood. The greatest prize may have eluded him, but Moss's place among the sport's legendary names was secured long before his enforced retirement.

Jonathan Palmer

Born 7 November 1956 (London)
Grand Prix starts: 84   Grand Prix victories: 0 - best result: 4th place, Australian GP 1987
Points total: 14

A career of outstanding early achievements but unfulfilled potential.

Jonathan Palmer qualified as a doctor before concentrating full-time on racing. He established his credentials in single-seaters in Formula Ford in the late 1970s, and in 1981 won the British Formula Three championship. The following year it was on to F2, and after a difficult year of adjusting to the step up in class Palmer won the European title in 1983, winning six of the twelve rounds. It was on the strength of these achievements that Palmer was invited to test for Williams. The team's driver line-up consisted of reigning champion Keke Rosberg and Jacques Laffite. Palmer was handed his F1 debut in a one-off drive at the 1983 European Grand Prix, held at Brands Hatch. His was the third works Williams that day, but he outperformed Laffite, who failed to qualify. Palmer finished 13th, having qualified 25th, a highly creditable first outing.

Success elusive in uncompetitive cars

1984 saw Palmer compete in his first full F1 championship, with RAM. There were five top-ten finishes and eight retirements. A move to Zakspeed, where he spent the following two seasons, barely improved his chances of getting into the points. Sports cars provided the highlights of this period, notably a second-place finish at Le Mans in 1985.

Winner of Jim Clark Cup

Palmer moved to Tyrrell in 1987, the start of a three-year association which proved more fruitful. He took 4th in Adelaide and was in the points at Monaco and Hockenheim to finish 11th in the title race. He also picked up the Jim Clark Cup, awarded to the best-placed non-turbocharged car in the championship. 1988 was an anticlimax, and in 1989 his form waned after Jean Alesi arrived on the team. He quit Grand Prix racing in 1990 to become test driver at McLaren, while continuing to compete in sports cars. After James Hunt's premature death in 1993 Palmer became one of the voices of motor

racing as co-commentator alongside Murray Walker. He went on to form his own junior single-seater championship, Formula Palmer Audi.

After some outstanding achievements early in his career, Palmer failed to realise his considerable potential. It remains a matter of conjecture what impact he might have made on F1 had he enjoyed the backing of one of the top teams of the day and driven a more competitive car.

Mike Parkes

24 September 1931 (Richmond, Surrey) - 28 August 1977
Grand Prix starts: 6   Grand Prix victories: 0 – best result: 2nd place, French GP 1966, Italian GP 1966
Points total: 14

A promising career halted by serious injury.

Few drivers make their Grand Prix debut with Ferrari, but circumstances conspired for Mike Parkes to do just that in 1966. He made a highly promising start – taking 2nd place in each of the two races he finished that year – but a horrific accident the following season meant that his great potential remained unfulfilled.

Parkes was born into the motoring world, the son of the chairman of Alvis, part of the Rootes group. He trained as an engineer with Rootes while competing in sports cars, where he enjoyed considerable success. He failed to qualify his Fry-Climax for the 1959 British Grand Prix, and again concentrated his efforts on sports car racing. Second place at Le Mans in 1961, where he partnered Willy Mairesse, impressed Enzo Ferrari sufficiently to offer him a place on the works team.

Surtees' departure provides big break
Parkes had to wait until 1966 to break into Grand Prix racing. The chance came when John Surtees quit the team, disillusioned over Ferrari's concentration on sports car events, which he felt was hampering his chance of a second world title. Parkes' debut came at Reims, the third round of the 1966 championship. He qualified 3rd and finished 2nd, a fine performance. Ferrari did not compete at Brands Hatch, preferring to focus on Le Mans. After failing to finish in the next two races, Parkes took pole at Monza, ahead of teammate Ludovico Scarfiotti. He led for several laps in the early stages but eventually brought the V12 Ferrari 312 home behind Scarfiotti, much to the delight of the home fans.

Severe injury ends F1 career
1967 began brightly, Parkes and Scarfiotti dead-heating in the non-championship Syracuse Grand Prix, and Parkes crossing the line first in the International Trophy at Silverstone. Parkes brought his Ferrari home in 4th place in his first championship race, Zandvoort. But in the next round, Spa, he crashed out on the first lap, sustaining severe leg injuries. He recovered and continued competing until 1973, but not at the top level, and he never recaptured his best form. Parkes returned to his roots as a first-rate engineer, working for Fiat and Lancia, but was killed in a road accident in 1977.

Mike Parkes and John Surtees (right).

Tom Pryce

11 June 1949 (Ruthin, Glamorgan) - 5 March 1977
Grand Prix starts: 42   Grand Prix victories: 0 – best result: 3rd place, Austrian GP 1975, Brazilian GP 1976
Points total: 19

A driver with star quality and scintillating ability.

In the mid-1970s Tom Pryce was widely tipped to be a future world champion contender. He had made his name in Formula Ford, then worked his way through the divisions to earn his break into F1 in 1974. Pryce made his Grand Prix debut at the Belgian GP with the Token team. Entry to the next race, Monaco, was turned down on grounds of inexperience, so Pryce competed in the F3 race instead and romped home. By the time he made his next GP appearance, at Zandvoort, he had signed for Shadow, with whom he spent the remainder of his brief career. At Silverstone that year Pryce put the Shadow DN3 5th on the grid and recorded his first finish, a creditable 8th place. At the Nurburgring in the next round Pryce notched his first championship point.

Stunning pole at Silverstone

1975 began well, with victory in the Race of Champions at Brands Hatch, a circuit he knew well from the days when he worked as a mechanic at the racing school there to help finance his early forays on the competition circuit. Pryce got into the points in both the Belgian and Dutch GPs, then took a stunning pole at Silverstone. He led briefly in a race that was run in appalling conditions. His Shadow was among the many involved in accidents, causing the race to be red-flagged. In his next three outings Pryce was in scintillating form, finishing 4th, 3rd and 6th to end the season in 10th place in the championship.

Killed in freak accident

In 1976 Pryce opened up where he left off, taking 3rd at Interlagos. Of the twelve races in which he went the distance that season, only once did he finish out of the top ten. He amassed two more points than the previous year, despite sponsorship problems which affected Shadow's financial health. Those difficulties had been solved by 1977 but Pryce was killed in the third championship race, Kyalami. In a bizarre incident, a marshal crossed the track to go to the assistance of Pryce's teammate, Renzo Zorzi, carrying a fire extinguisher in case the Shadow DN8 burst into flames before the driver could get clear. At that moment Pryce crested the brow of the hill and had no time to avoid the marshal, who was killed instantly. The fire extinguisher struck Pryce in the head, and a driver of star quality lost his life, aged just 27.

Tom Pryce (Shadow DN5B Ford) in 8th position at the German Grand Prix, Nurburgring, in 1975.

Mike Spence

30 December 1936 (Croydon, Surrey) - 7 May 1968
Grand Prix starts: 36   Grand Prix victories: 0 – best result: 3rd place, Mexican GP 1965
Points total: 27

The consistent and talented Spence meets disaster at Indianapolis.

Mike Spence was a highly talented driver who made his mark in the late 1950s, competing in his father's Turner sports car and latterly an AC Bristol. He entered Formula Junior in 1960 and made his F1 debut the following year in a works Emeryson at the non-championship Solitude Grand Prix. He drove a Lotus in the 1962 Formula Junior series, impressing enough to land a contract with Team Lotus the following season.

1963 saw him compete mainly in Formula Junior, but his Grand Prix chance came when Trevor Taylor was injured just before Monza. He ran well on his championship debut before his Lotus-Climax failed.

Victory in F2 championship

Jim Clark and Peter Arundell spearheaded Lotus' 1964 campaign, leaving Spence to compete predominantly in F2, winning the British championship for Team Lotus. In July of that year he was promoted again after Arundell was badly injured in an F2 race at Reims. He competed in the last six championship races of the season, his best showing being a 4th place in Mexico – ahead of Clark – and 6th at Monza.

In his final season with Lotus Spence claimed 3rd spot in Mexico and was also in the points in South Africa and at Silverstone. Ten points gave him 8th place in the 1965 championship, level with Bruce McLaren. He also won the non-championship Race of Champions at Brands Hatch that year.

Great consistency

Spence joined BRM in 1966 but had to wait a year before securing a place in the team's Grand Prix line-up, where he partnered Jackie Stewart. Of the six races in which he made it to the finishing line Spence was in the points on five occasions, showing a fine level of consistency. The signs going into 1968 were promising. However, his

last championship race was to be New Year's Day, the South African GP. Two years earlier he had won the race when it didn't feature on the championship calendar. It was a retirement this time, his 37th and final GP start. On 7 May Spence was testing a Lotus 56 turbine car at Indianapolis, taking the place of Jim Clark, who had lost his life at Hockenheim the previous month. Having taken the STP Lotus round the banked track at a shade under 170mph – the second fastest lap ever – the car hit a wall and Spence was struck in the head by a flying wheel. He never regained consciousness.

Jackie Stewart

Born 11 June 1939 (Milton, Dunbartonshire)
Grand Prix starts: 99   Grand Prix victories: 27   Points total: 360
World Champion 1969, 1971, 1973

Utterly focused and clinically efficient Stewart won twenty-seven Grands Prix and three world crowns.

Jackie Stewart was a natural behind the wheel. He eased the car round the track with finesse and clinical efficiency, seeing everything that mattered, blocking out any extraneous sensory information. This ability to become detached and utterly focused brought Stewart 27 GP victories, setting a record that would not be beaten for fourteen years.

Stewart was a keen footballer and international-class clay pigeon shooter, but motor sport was in the blood: his father had been a TT rider in the 1930s and his elder brother, Jimmy, was a racing driver. In the 1950s the starstruck young Jackie followed Jimmy round the country, where he would seek autographs from the heroes of the day.

Tyrrell signs Stewart for F3

Stewart came relatively late to the sport; he was 21 before he first took to the wheel of a racing car. After winning races in 1961 and 1962 he joined the Ecurie Ecosse team, where he continued to impress. Ken Tyrrell spotted Stewart's burgeoning talent and invited him to test a Formula Three car at Goodwood, his first experience in a single-seater. In 1964 he won regularly in that division and in Formula Two.

It was with BRM that Stewart made his Grand Prix debut, finishing 6th in South Africa, the opening round of the 1965 championship. After three 2nd places – all to Jim Clark – he notched his first victory at Monza on 12 September. This outstanding rookie season at the top level saw him finish 3rd, behind Clark and teammate Graham Hill.

In the following two seasons BRM became increasingly uncompetitive and unreliable. After winning the opening round of the 1966 championship, Monaco, Stewart was involved in a huge first-lap pile-up at Spa. He was trapped for some time, semi-conscious and soaked in fuel. When he recovered he was at the forefront of the campaign to make F1 a safer sport.

Record victory at Nurburgring

For 1968 Stewart signed for Matra-Ford, where he was reunited with Tyrrell. He broke a bone in his hand in an F2 race early in the season but drove through the pain barrier to put himself in title contention. The highlight was a four-minute victory over Hill at the Nurburgring, the biggest winning margin in championship history. He went into the final race, Mexico, vying with Hill for the title, with reigning champion Denny Hulme also in with a chance. Retirement meant that he had to settle for 2nd place.

1969 saw Stewart go one better, sweeping to the

By the time Stewart walked away, his place in the sport's hall of fame had been long since secured.

championship with six wins in the eleven-race series. It could have been even more emphatic had his driveshaft not broken while leading at Monaco, while gearbox trouble in Germany restricted him to 2nd place. He clinched the title at Monza, crossing the line a whisker ahead of Rindt, Beltoise and McLaren, 0.2 sec. separating all four in one of the closest finishes ever.

Championship secured after eight rounds

1970 was a disappointment, as the new March chassis couldn't live with Lotus or Ferrari. But the following year Stewart sealed the title after just eight rounds, scoring six more wins along the way. He claimed his second title after a retirement in Austria, as the only men who could catch him, Ickx and Peterson, failed to score.

There were four more wins in 1972 but this time it was only good enough for 2nd place to Emerson Fittipaldi.

On 3 June 1973 Stewart won at Monaco to equal Clark's record of 25 victories. Four races later, Zandvoort, he set a new mark, and also won in Germany. However, probably the greatest drive of this, his third championship-winning season, came at Monza, where tyre problems left him down the field in 20th place but he carved his way through the field to finish 4th, a marvellous achievement.

Jackie Stewart with Graham Hill.

Jackie Stewart (Matra MS10 Ford) in third
position in the 1968 French Grand Prix,
Rouen-les-Essarts.

Stewart walks away after Cevert's death

Going into the final race, Watkins Glen, Stewart's
record stood at 27 wins from 99 GP starts. He had long
been harbouring thoughts of retirement, and intended
to bow out after his 100th race. But when teammate
François Cevert was killed in practice the Tyrrell team
withdrew and 34-year-old Stewart walked away, his
place in the sport's hall of fame long since secured.

Even though his driving days were over, Stewart
continued to be one of motor racing's greatest
ambassadors. In 1996 he fulfilled another ambition
when, along with son Paul, he formed his own F1 team.
Winning driver became victorious team owner when
Johnny Herbert won the 1999 European GP for
Stewart Grand Prix.

John Surtees

Born 11 February 1934 (Tatsfield, Surrey)
Grand Prix starts: 111   Grand Prix victories: 6   Points total: 180
World Champion 1964

The only man to reach the pinnacle of achievement as both rider and driver.

Many have made the transition from two- to four-wheel racing, but John Surtees remains the only man to have reached the pinnacle in both sports. Bikes were his first love, a passion inherited from his father, who had a motorcycle shop in Forest Hill, London, and who also competed at a modest level. Surtees entered his first bike race when he was 15, notched his first victory the following year and in the early 1950s was winning regularly at meetings up and down the country. His big break came in 1955, when he joined the MV Agusta team. A year later he claimed the first of his four 500cc championships, and in the following three seasons he made it a double by also winning the world title in the 350cc class. There was also a hat-trick of wins in the 500cc Isle of Man TT.

Fresh challenge

By the late 1950s Surtees was seeking a fresh challenge. He joined Ken Tyrrell's Formula Junior team to gain some four-wheel experience and took to it immediately. At Goodwood on Easter Monday 1960 he finished second to Jim Clark after a thrilling duel. Colin Chapman offered him a Formula One drive when he could fit it into his schedule. And what a schedule. That year saw Surtees compete in – and win – the 350cc and 500cc world championships, interspersed with Formula Junior and Formula Two races. And there were four Grands Prix as well. The first of those, Monaco on 29 May, ended with transmission failure, but six weeks later at Silverstone he brought his Lotus Climax home second to the man poised to take the world title, Jack Brabham. He then took pole at the Portuguese Grand Prix and led by some distance before his car again failed.

Overtures from Ferrari rejected

Understandably, Chapman wanted to retain Surtees' services for 1961 but with Jim Clark and Innes Ireland already on the Lotus team there was political tension and Surtees pre-empted the situation and withdrew. With few openings available he signed for Yeoman Credit Cooper, an uncompetitive outfit. The season yielded just four

Surtees claims the '64 world crown from Hill by a single point.

championship points, yet Surtees' obvious talent brought Enzo Ferrari knocking at his door. He declined the overture, feeling he wasn't yet ready for such a move. He drove for Lola in 1962, and 2nd places in both Britain and Germany helped him to 4th place in the championship. Ferrari renewed their interest and this time Surtees decided the time was right.

His first Grand Prix victory came in his sixth race for Ferrari, at the Nurburgring, on 4 August 1963, where he came out on top after a terrific battle with Jim Clark. There were a number of retirements thereafter and Surtees finished the season on 22 points and another 4th place.

John Surtees (Lola Mk4 Climax) in fourth position in the1962 Monaco Grand Prix, Monte Carlo.

Delirious scenes after Monza victory

For 1964 Ferrari developed a new V8 engine, yet there were retirements in three of the first four races. The sixth round brought a stunning victory at the Nurburgring, Surtees twice breaking the lap record on his way to victory. This continued his phenomenal scoring record: only once when his car made it to the finishing line had he finished out of the points in a Grand Prix.

When the Ferrari limped out at Zeltweg with suspension trouble Surtees thought his championship hopes had gone. But with his two main rivals, Clark and Hill, also failing to finish, at least his arrears were no worse. Victory at Monza naturally prompted scenes of hysteria, and with Hill and Clark again missing out, the championship was again alive. Surtees finished 2nd to Hill in the penultimate round, Watkins Glen, and went to Mexico trailing the 1962 champion by five points. Clark also had a chance of retaining his crown. The permutations were complex, but Surtees was the only one of the three to have it in his own hands: victory and the title were his.

Snatches title from Hill

Hill's chance of improving on his 39 points came to an end when his BRM collided with the Ferrari of Surtees' stablemate Lorenzo Bandini. Clark had built up a handsome lead and was set to win the championship unless Surtees – running 4th – could take 2nd spot.

Clark's Lotus sprang an oil leak with a lap to go, leaving Dan Gurney in front, followed by Bandini and Surtees. Had this order been maintained Hill would have won the title, but Bandini allowed his teammate to ease through into 2nd place – thereby clinching the championship from Hill by a single point.

Surtees suffered serious injury in the 1965 CanAm race, but recovered for the start of the 1966 season. He won the second round, Spa, but then walked out on Ferrari after a row with team boss Eugenio Dragoni. He finished the season with Cooper, winning the Mexican Grand Prix with his new team and finishing the season a creditable runner-up.

Team Surtees forms

Surtees spent the next two years helping Honda to establish a foothold in Formula One. The highlight of this period came at Monza 1967, when he snatched a dramatic last-lap victory from Brabham, crossing the line 0.2 seconds ahead of the reigning champion.

After an unhappy year with BRM in 1969 Surtees, a gifted engineer and meticulous organiser, formed his own team. He continued to drive for two years before stepping down to concentrate on running Team Surtees. The outfit folded in 1978, Surtees the team boss not managing to scale the heights he had as both rider and driver.

Derek Warwick

Born 27 August 1954 (Alresford, Hampshire)
Grand Prix starts: 147   Grand Prix victories: 0 - best result: 2nd place Belgian GP 1984, British GP 1984
Points total: 71

With better luck Britain could have been acclaiming Warwick as its seventh world champion.

In the early 1980s Derek Warwick was considered a better prospect than Nigel Mansell. With better luck Britain could have been acclaiming Warwick as its seventh world champion. Warwick cut his teeth in stock cars, taking the World Superstox title in 1972. He moved to single-seaters with Formula Ford, where he won a phenomenal 31 races from 63 starts. Next came Formula Three, and in only his second season he won the Vandervell F3 crown, beating future world champion Nelson Piquet.

Steps up to F1 with Toleman

In 1979 Warwick contested the F2 championship, and secured a place with the Toleman team for the following year. Toleman entered Formula One in 1981, but it wasn't until the final round that Warwick managed to qualify the TG181.

1982 showed marginal improvement, but it was the following season's Dutch GP before Warwick notched his and Toleman's first championship points.

Passes up chance to join Williams

For 1984 Warwick moved to Renault. Four podium finishes put him 7th in the championship, but it was to prove a false dawn. Renault was in decline, yet Warwick opted to remain, passing up the chance to join a team on the up, Williams. Warwick notched just two 5th places in 1985 to finish 26 points behind the Briton who had opted to join Williams, Nigel Mansell.

Senna vetoed the decision for Warwick to join Lotus in 1986, not wanting a driver of equal status who would dilute his own chances. Elio de Angelis' death created an opening at Brabham, and Warwick returned to F1, but he failed to get in the points with a notoriously difficult car.

In 1987 he moved to Arrows, where he would remain for three seasons. Initially the car was running an outdated BMW engine and Warwick was placed just once.

Costly pit stop delays

Four 4th places helped him to 7th in the 1988 championship, and the following year there was a new Ross Brawn-designed car. Warwick might have won in Brazil but for two disastrous pit stops, and he also led in Canada before his engine blew, but the season fizzled out thereafter.

1990 saw him join Lotus, but the move came too late. Senna had left in '87, seeing that he could go no further with that team. While the Brazilian was winning the 1990 world title with McLaren, Warwick managed just one 5th place with Lotus. He later said that in an effort to get the maximum from an indifferent car he took more risks that season than ever before.

Warwick quit F1 at the end of the year, choosing to contest the world sports car championship with Jaguar. He returned briefly in 1993 with the Footwork team but scored just four points.

John Watson

Born 4 May 1946, (Belfast, Northern Ireland)
Grand Prix starts: 152   Grand Prix victories: 5   Points total: 169

Runner-up Watson was not always rewarded with the points he deserved.

John Watson began his racing career in an Austin-Healey Sprite in 1963. He impressed after moving to single-seaters in the Irish Formule Libre series, and by 1970 he was contesting the F2 championship in an outdated Brabham BT30, regularly outperforming works drivers.

Ecclestone hands Watson F1 debut

His F1 debut came in the non-championship John Player Trophy race at Brands Hatch in 1972, where he finished sixth in a March. This, together with some eye-catching performances in F2, prompted Brabham boss Bernie Ecclestone to hand Watson his Grand Prix debut at Silverstone, 14 July 1973.

1974 saw Watson contest his first full GP season in a private Brabham with the Goldie Hexagon team. He notched his first point by finishing 6th at Monaco, and had two more top-six finishes in the new Brabham BT44.

Watson signed for Team Surtees in 1975 but the season was bedevilled by mechanical problems, and he couldn't coax the TS16 into the points in any of the GPs. Surtees withdrew, and Watson ended the year with Penske.

Austrian GP yields first victory

Watson scored his maiden victory in the 1976 Austrian GP, and podium finishes in France and Britain earned Watson seventh place in the championship. Penske withdrew at the end of the year and the Ulsterman returned to Brabham. His form over the next two years was not always rewarded with the points it deserved. In the 1977 French GP he led for 75 of the 80 laps before running out of fuel with victory in sight. The following year saw a marked improvement, 25 points and 6th in the championship, his best season to date.

Watson joins McLaren

In 1979 Watson moved to a McLaren team in transition, and two seasons yielded just 21 points. Ron Dennis took over in 1980, and designer John Barnard produced the first carbon fibre F1 car. Watson drove the

MP4/1 to victory at Silverstone in 1981, but it was the following year when he came closest to winning the title. Victories at Zolder and Detroit meant a showdown in Las Vegas. Needing a win, Watson could only manage second, and Williams' Keke Rosberg lifted the title.

1983 was Watson's swansong year in F1. The era of the turbo had arrived, and with McLaren still running the Ford DFV, Watson slipped to 6th in the championship. The highlight came at Long Beach, where he scored his 5th and final victory from 22nd on the grid.

Watson was replaced by Prost in 1984, and apart from a one-off drive for McLaren in the 1985 European GP, he concentrated his efforts on sports cars. He established a racing school at Silverstone and also forged a new career as a TV commentator.

Acknowledgements

Thanks to everyone at LAT especially Peter Higham, Tim Wright,
Kevin Wood, Zoë Mayho and the digital team John Tingle,
Tim Clarke and Alastair Staley.

Thanks also to Vicki Harris, Alison Gauntlett and John Dunne